Princess Jaida's Quarantine Birthday

Copyright © 2020 Jaida Lopez

ISBN 9781513665856

All rights reserved. No part of this book may be used or reproduced by any means, graphic, electronic or mechanical, including photocopying, recording, taping or by information storage retrieval system without the written permission of the publisher except in the case of brief quotation embodied in critical articles and reviews.

Cover & Book Illustrations by Arsalan

Book Published by Shekinah Glory Publishing

www.shekinahglorypublishing.org

(936) 314-7458

Dedication

I would like to dedicate my book to the following special individuals:
My Grandma Bernice - Thank you for my mommy.
My cousin Janovia.
My First Niece Khloe and to your beautiful mother Sha-Asia, who is now an angel watching over us. #justiceforSha-Asia

Acknowledgements

I would like to acknowledge the following special individuals:

My Mommy – Thank you for being my biggest fan. I love you!

My Papi – Thank you for allowing me to be as silly as I want to be.

My Brothers Jahad & Jaquis – Thank you for making sure I go to school EVERYDAY. (I know I'm pocket)

Last but not least, my family and friends – Thank you for ALWAYS supporting me, no matter what.

I love you!

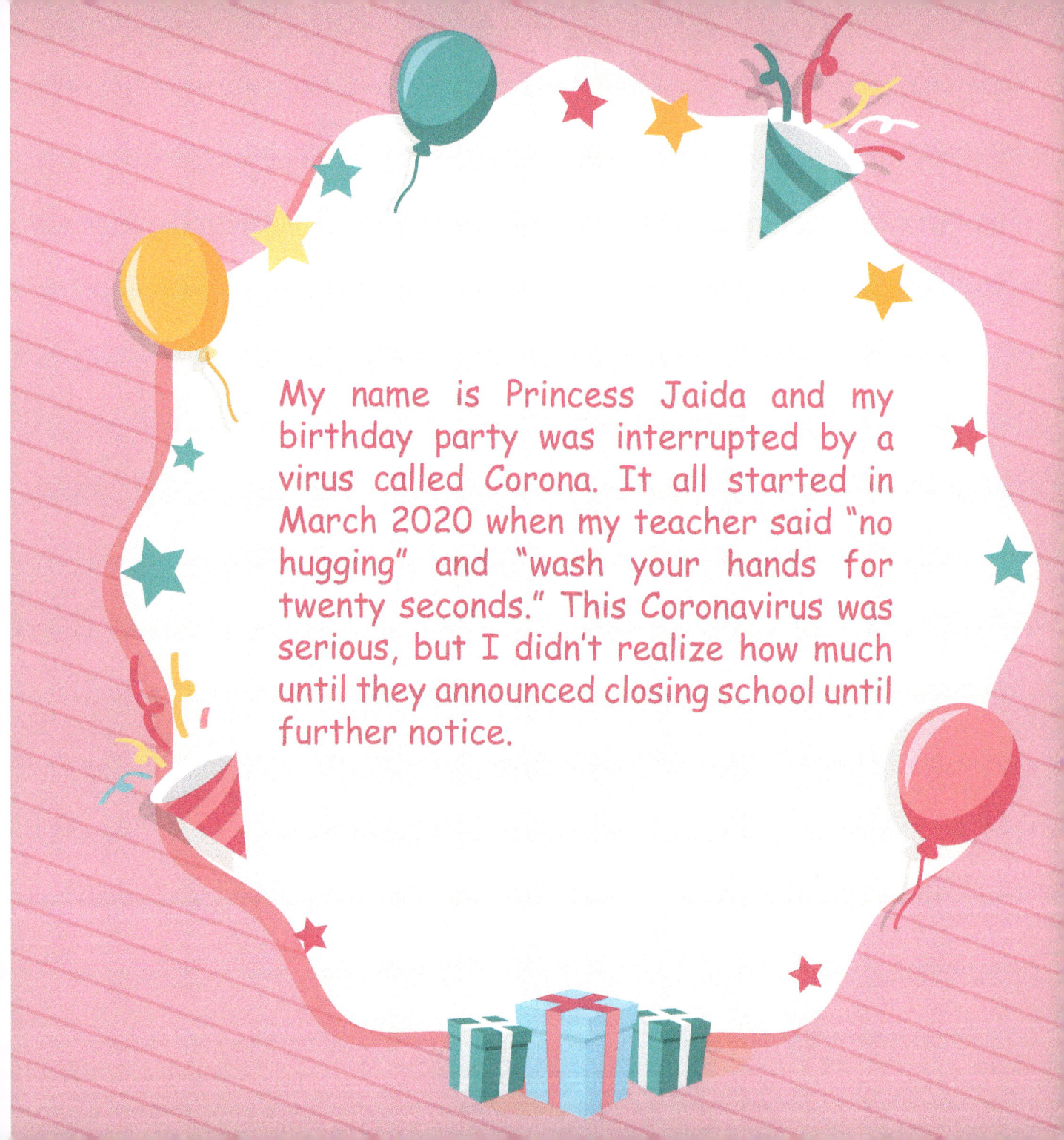

My name is Princess Jaida and my birthday party was interrupted by a virus called Corona. It all started in March 2020 when my teacher said "no hugging" and "wash your hands for twenty seconds." This Coronavirus was serious, but I didn't realize how much until they announced closing school until further notice.

Days passed, no school! Weeks passed, still, no school! I was counting down the days while keeping up with the calendar on my iPad. I stayed busy with TikTok and watching my favorite show Grace's World.

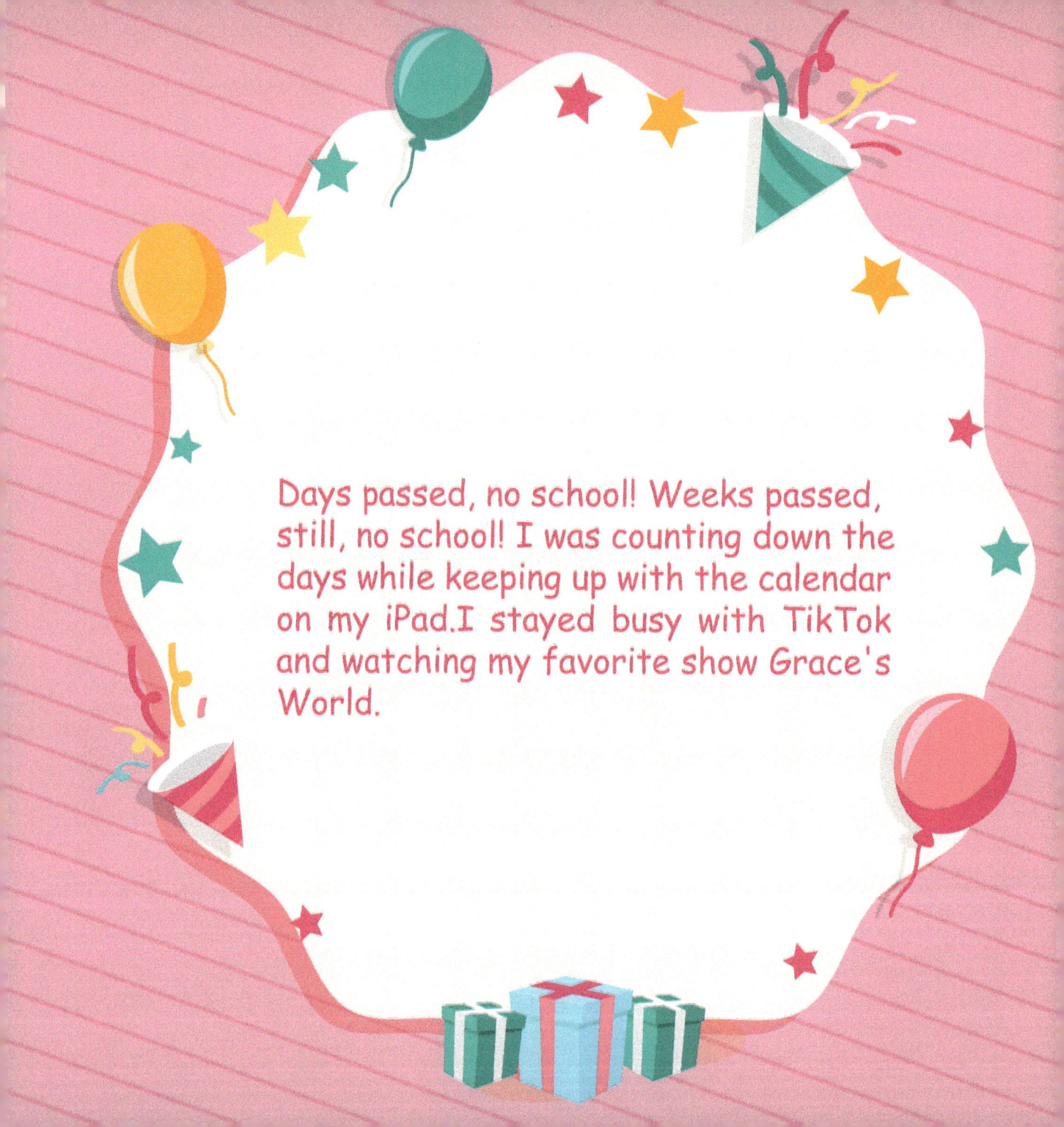

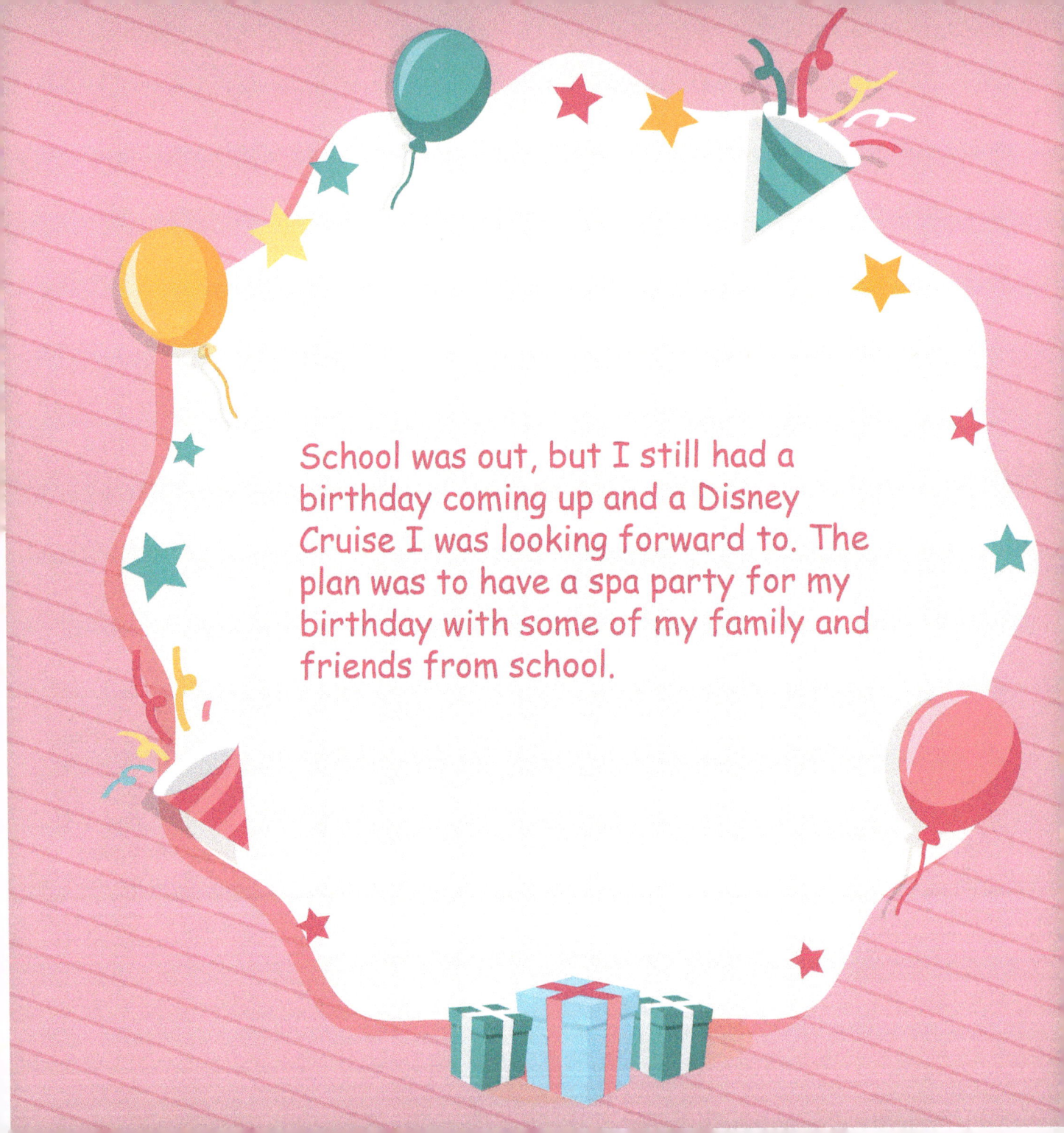

School was out, but I still had a birthday coming up and a Disney Cruise I was looking forward to. The plan was to have a spa party for my birthday with some of my family and friends from school.

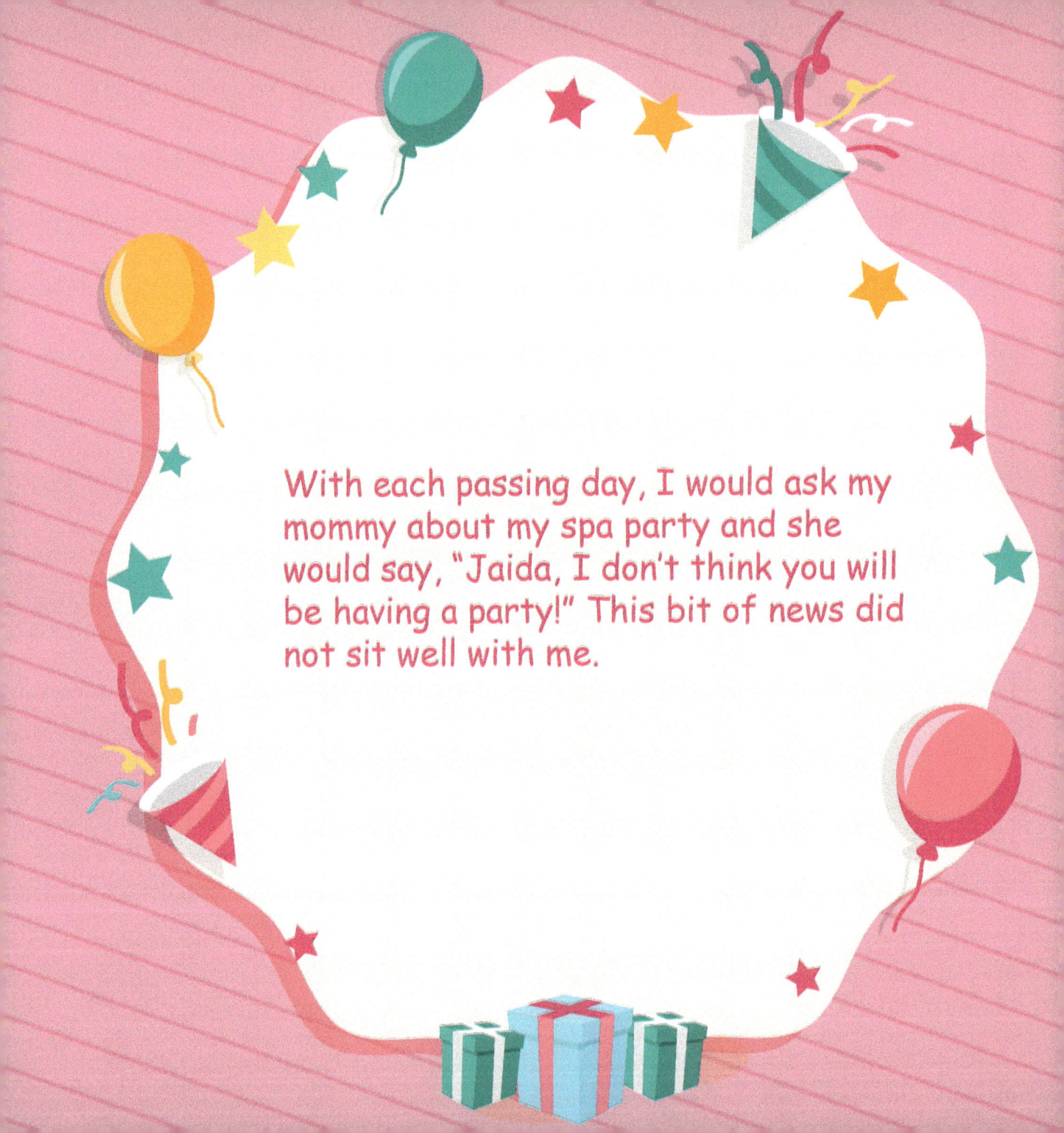

With each passing day, I would ask my mommy about my spa party and she would say, "Jaida, I don't think you will be having a party!" This bit of news did not sit well with me.

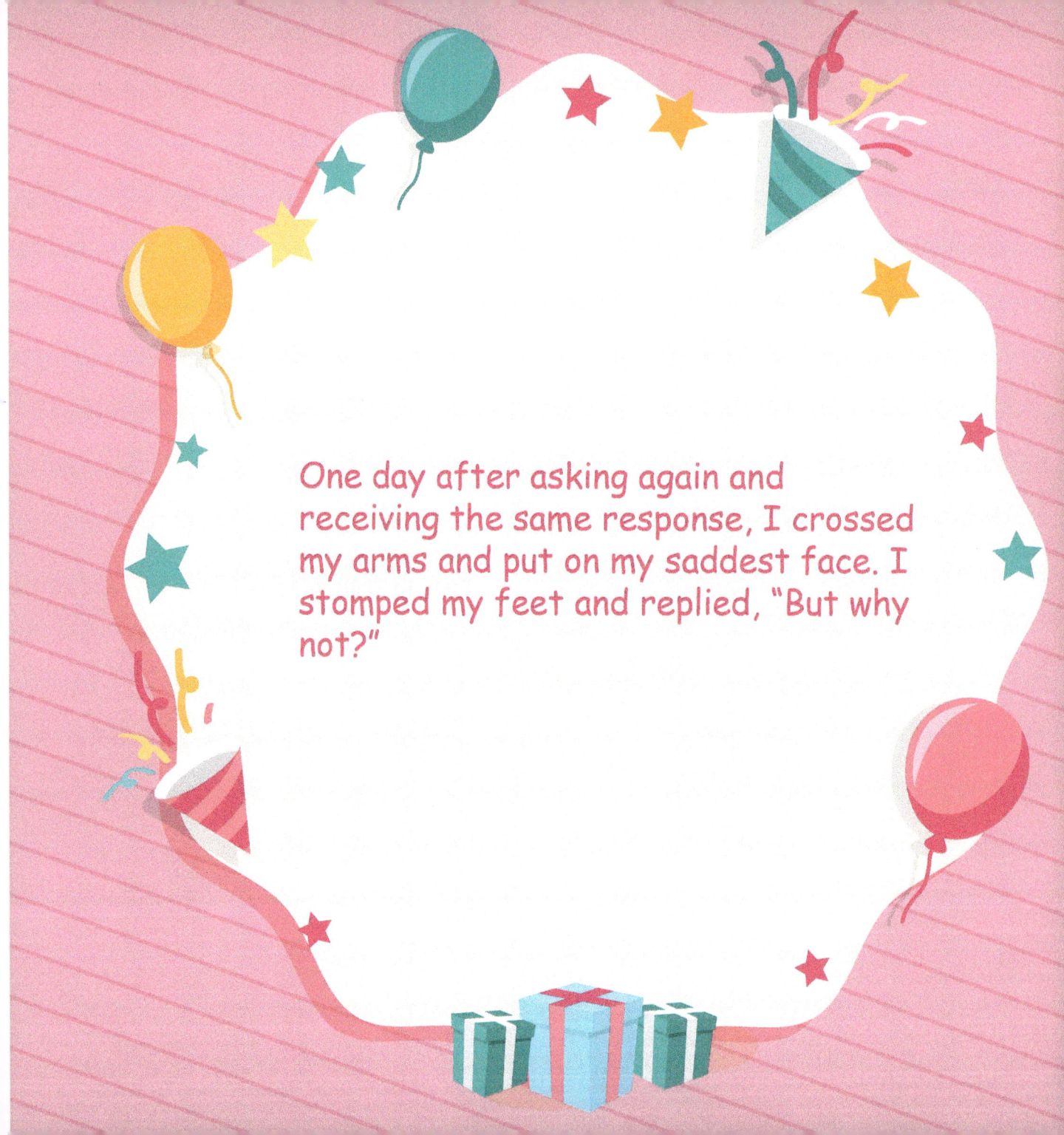

One day after asking again and receiving the same response, I crossed my arms and put on my saddest face. I stomped my feet and replied, "But why not?"

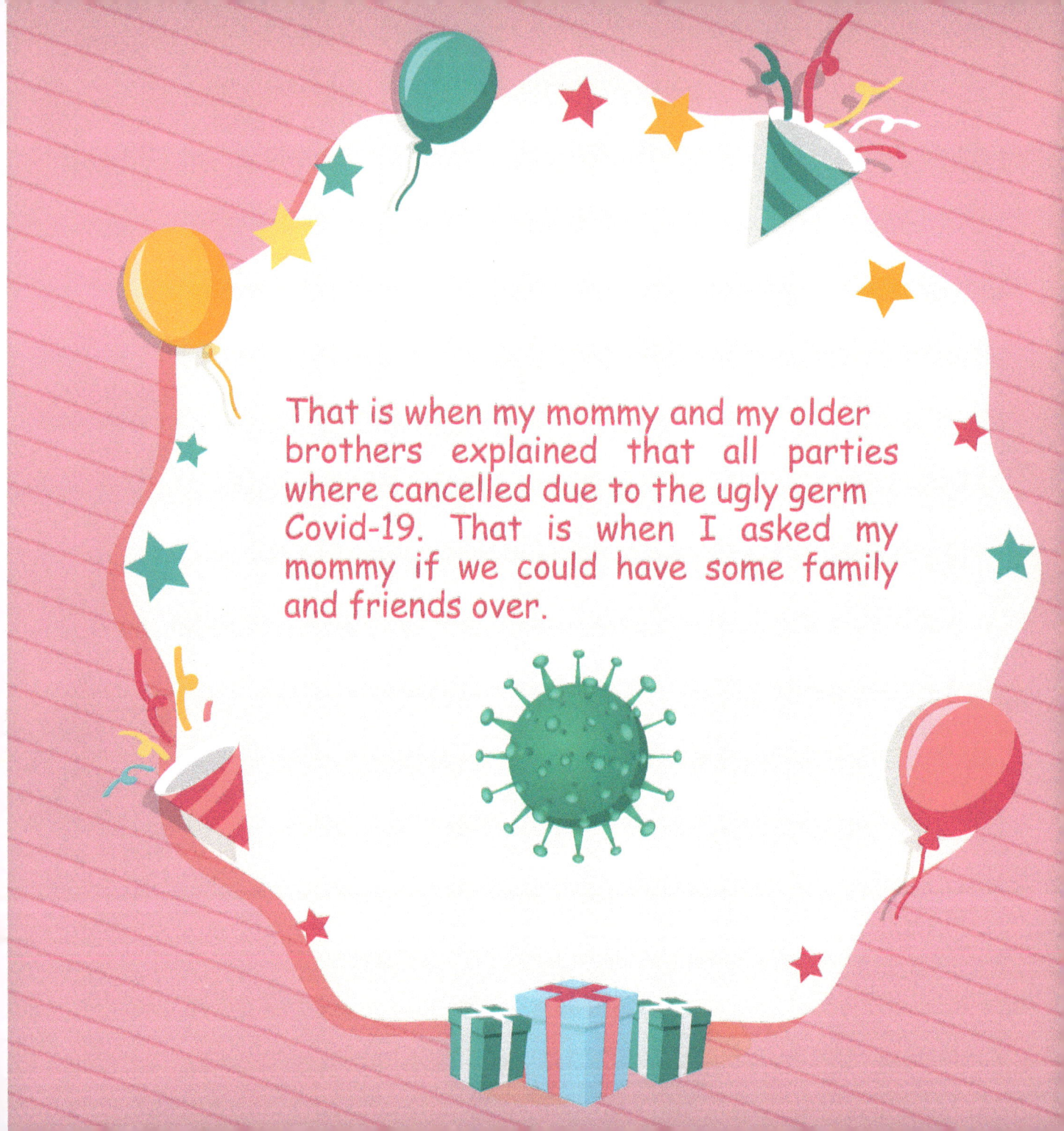

That is when my mommy and my older brothers explained that all parties where cancelled due to the ugly germ Covid-19. That is when I asked my mommy if we could have some family and friends over.

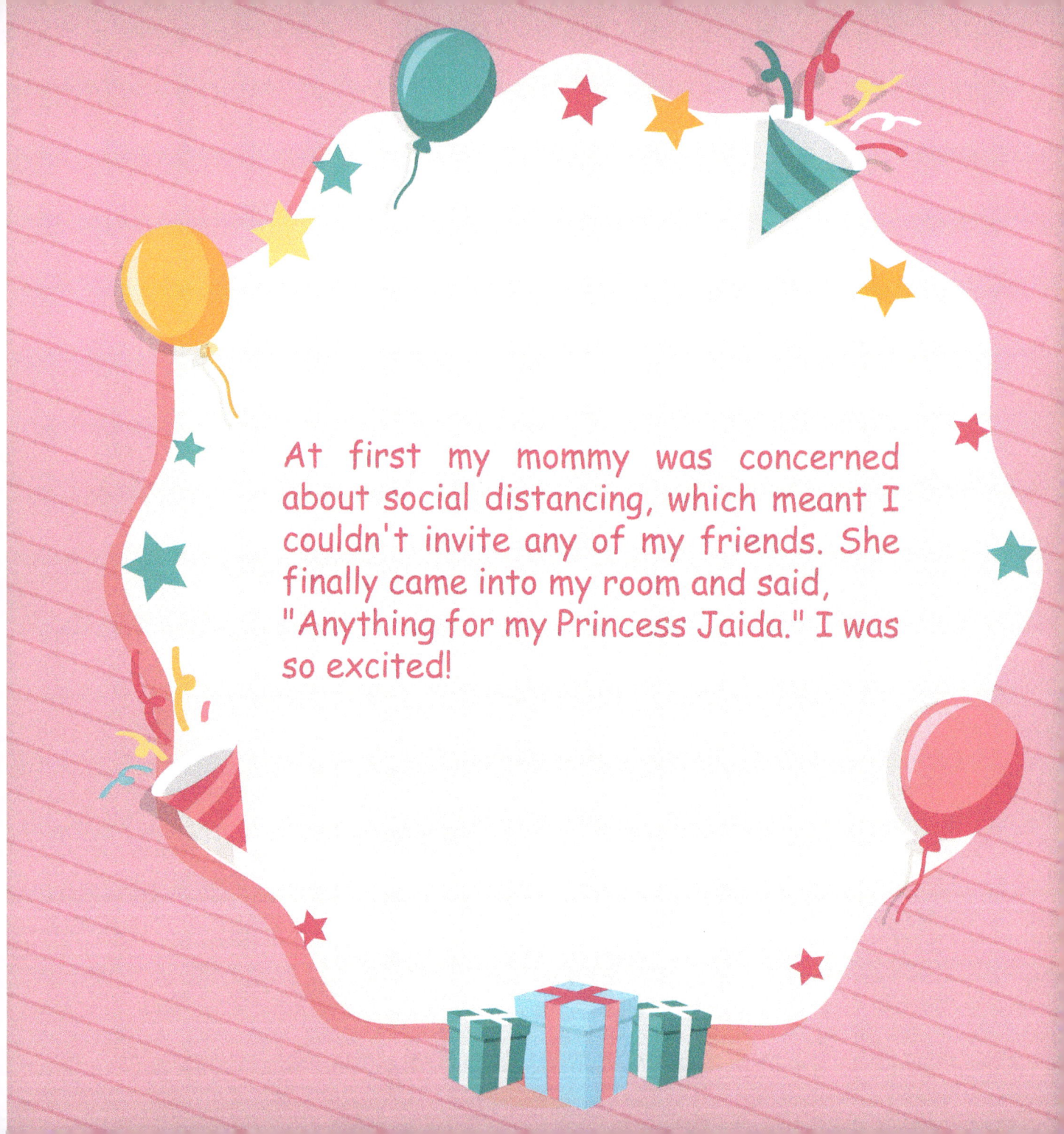

At first my mommy was concerned about social distancing, which meant I couldn't invite any of my friends. She finally came into my room and said, "Anything for my Princess Jaida." I was so excited!

I jumped into Princess Jaida's party planning mode. I LOVE pizza, so the menu would consist of hot cheesy pizza, cake, and my favorite ice cream.

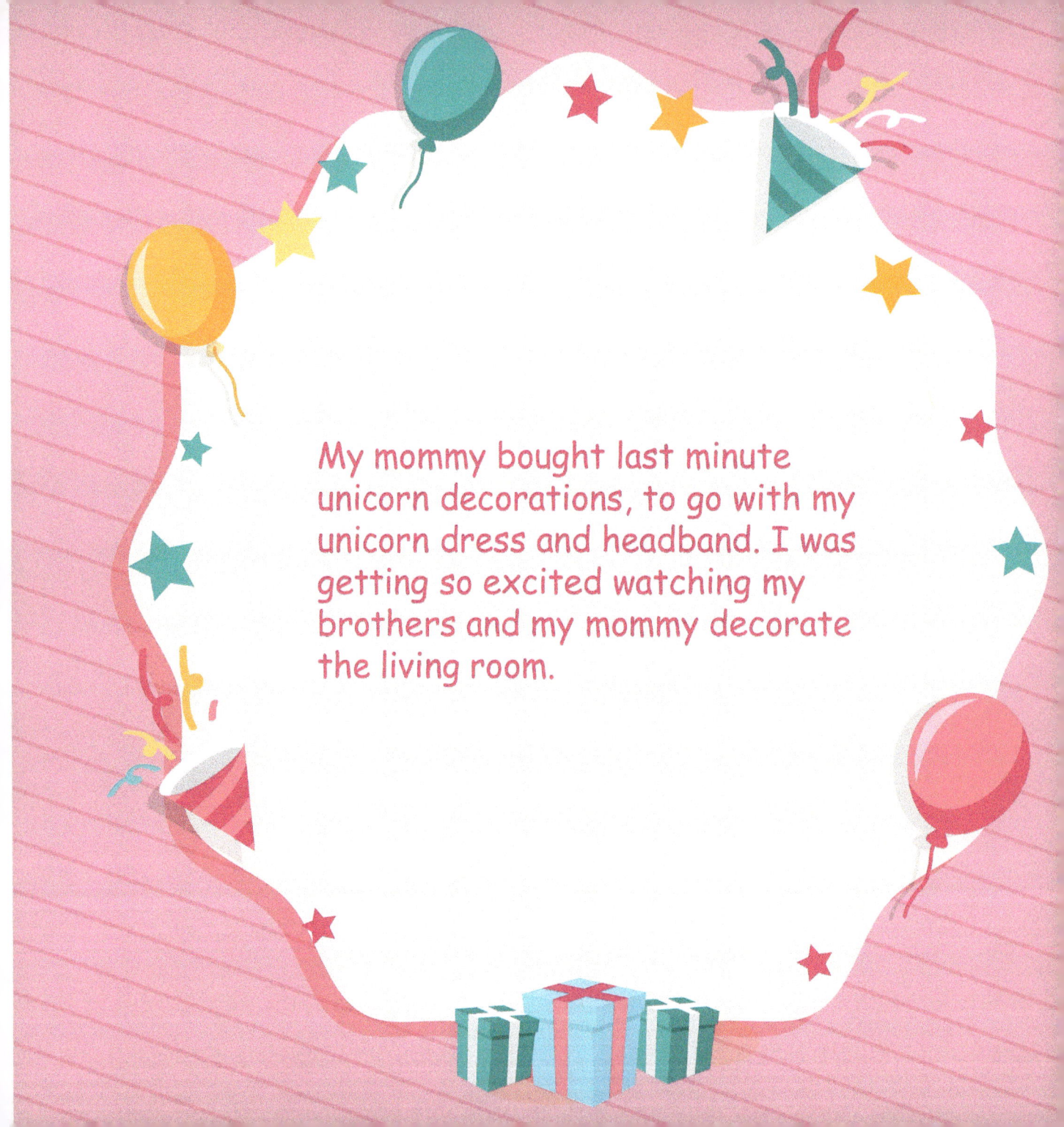

My mommy bought last minute unicorn decorations, to go with my unicorn dress and headband. I was getting so excited watching my brothers and my mommy decorate the living room.

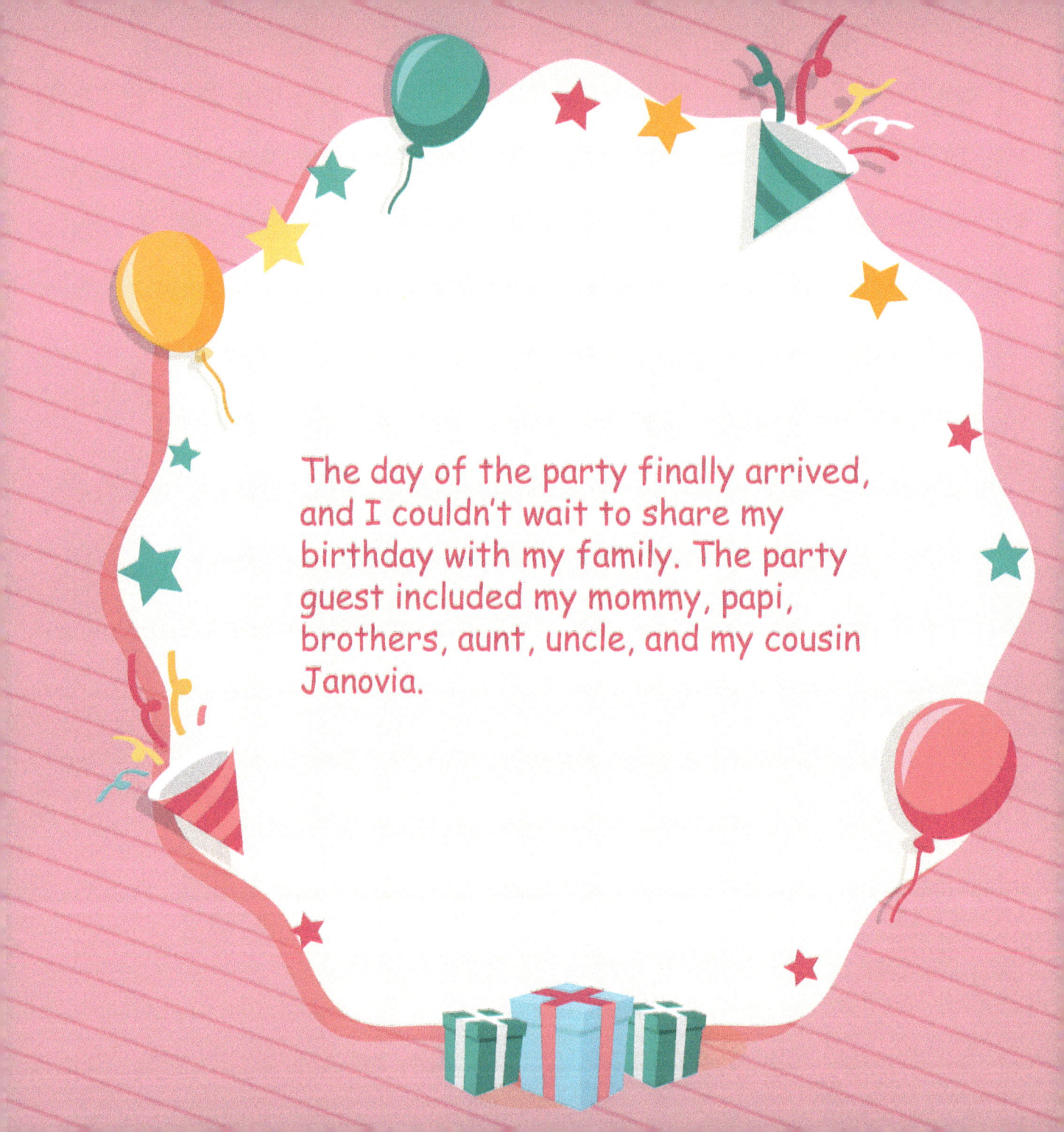

The day of the party finally arrived, and I couldn't wait to share my birthday with my family. The party guest included my mommy, papi, brothers, aunt, uncle, and my cousin Janovia.

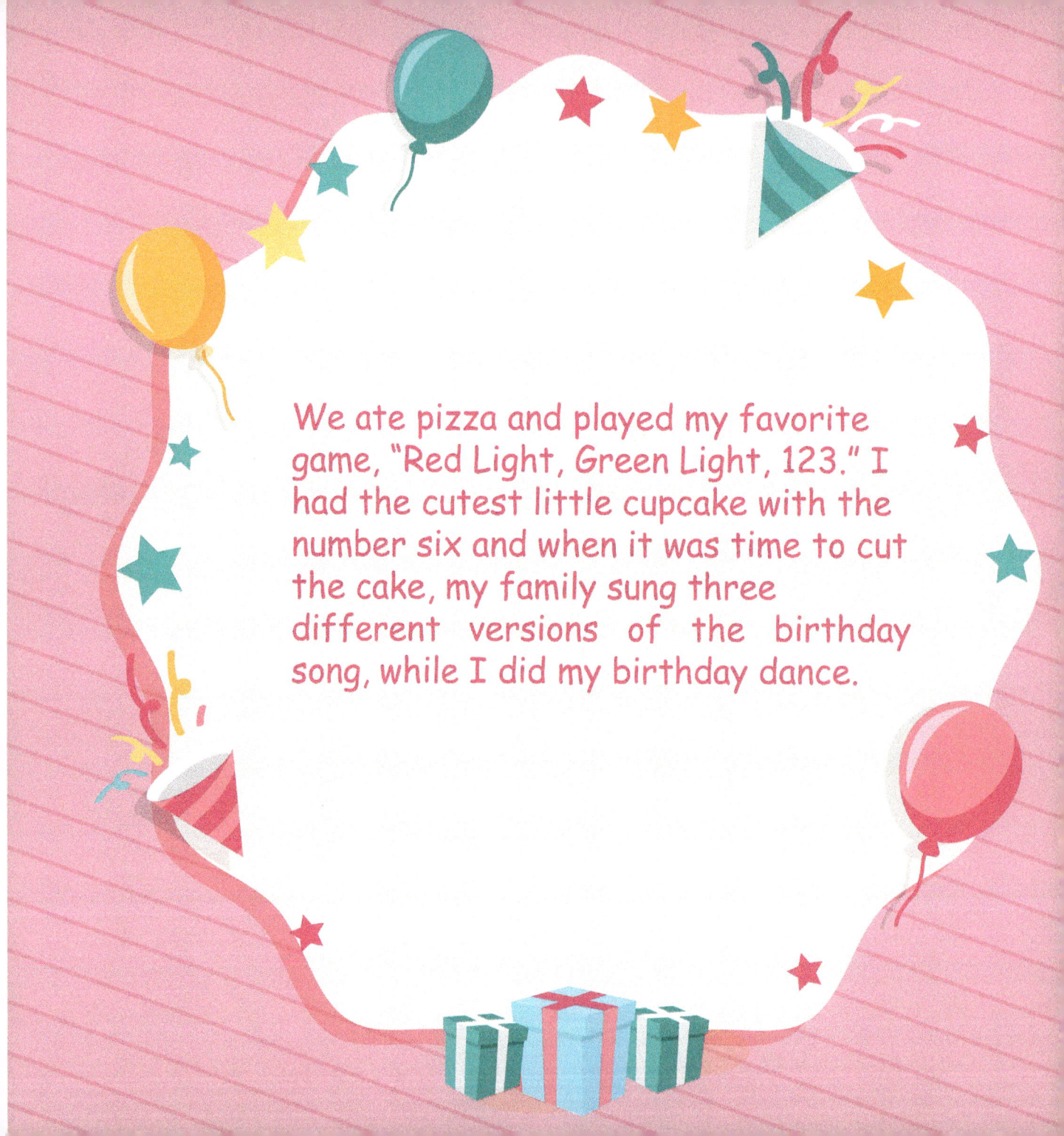

We ate pizza and played my favorite game, "Red Light, Green Light, 123." I had the cutest little cupcake with the number six and when it was time to cut the cake, my family sung three different versions of the birthday song, while I did my birthday dance.

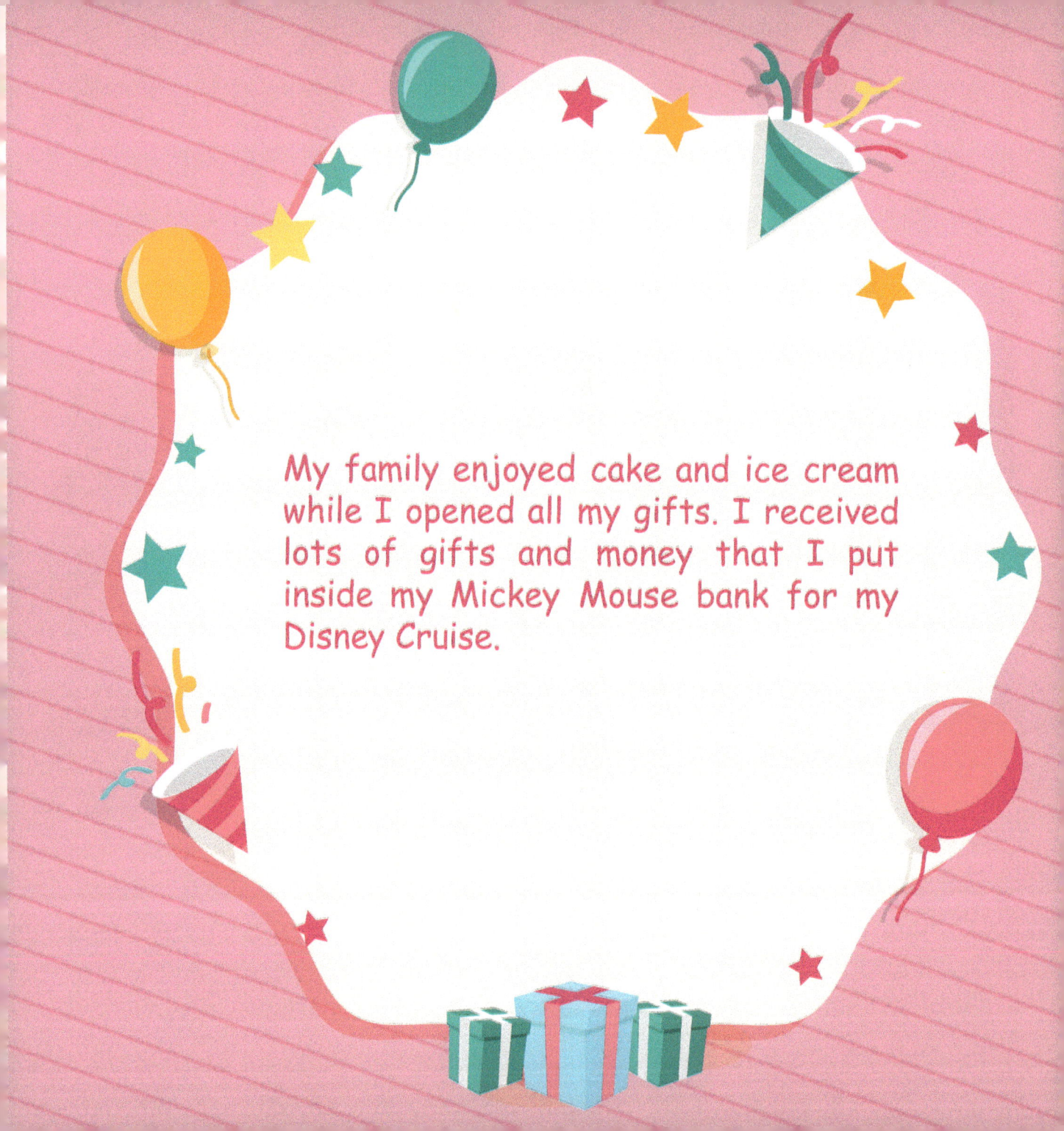

My family enjoyed cake and ice cream while I opened all my gifts. I received lots of gifts and money that I put inside my Mickey Mouse bank for my Disney Cruise.

"WAIT!! My Disney Cruise!! "Mommy are we still going on the Disney ship?" I asked. She replied, "No Princess Jaida, the Disney ship is closed, but you can keep saving your money and God willing we can go next year."

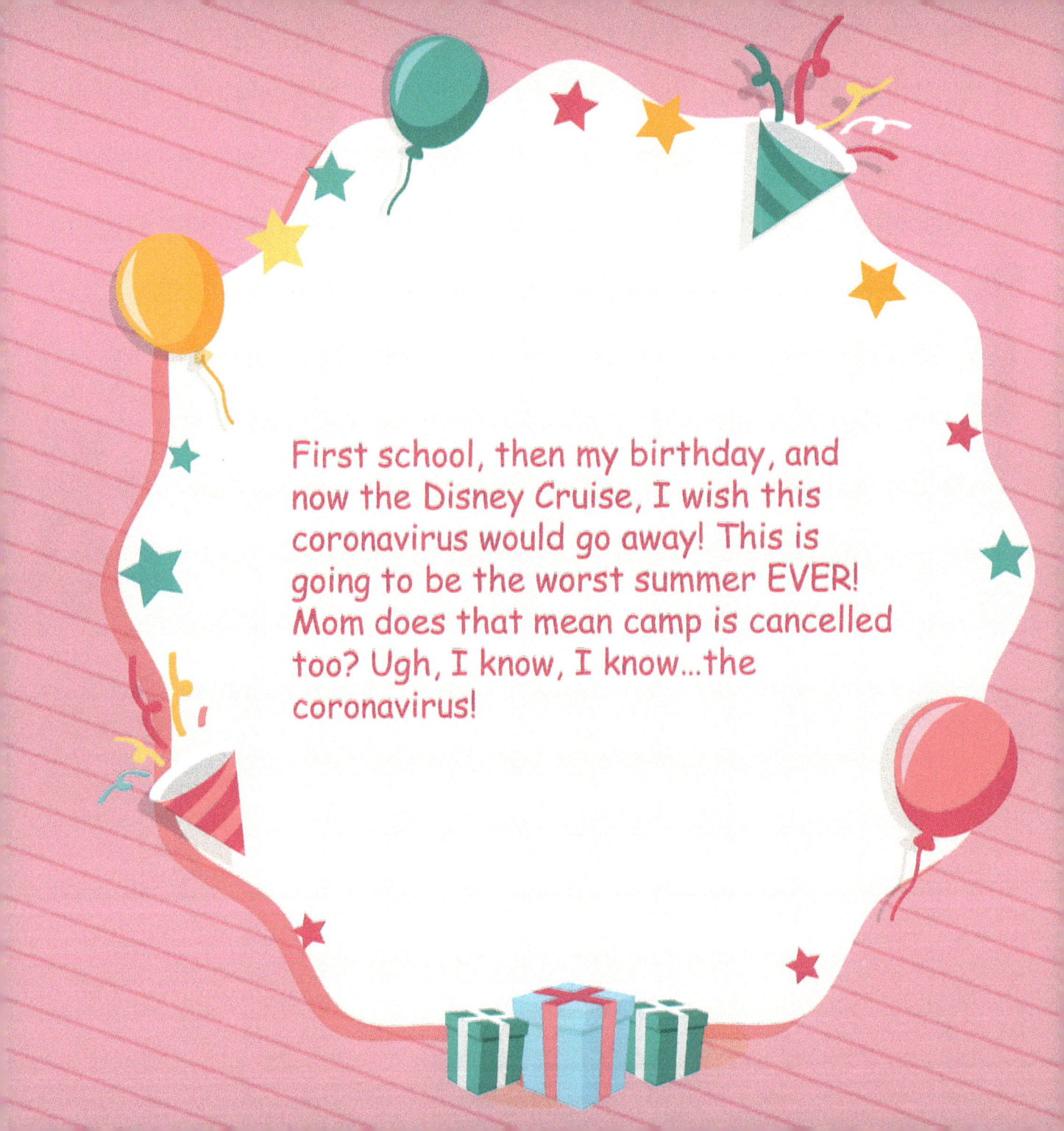

First school, then my birthday, and now the Disney Cruise, I wish this coronavirus would go away! This is going to be the worst summer EVER! Mom does that mean camp is cancelled too? Ugh, I know, I know...the coronavirus!

From the Heart of Princess Jaida

I would like to acknowledge all of the essential workers who have sacrificed selflessly during this pandemic. Thank you so much, for it not only affected you and many others, but it affected the little people too.

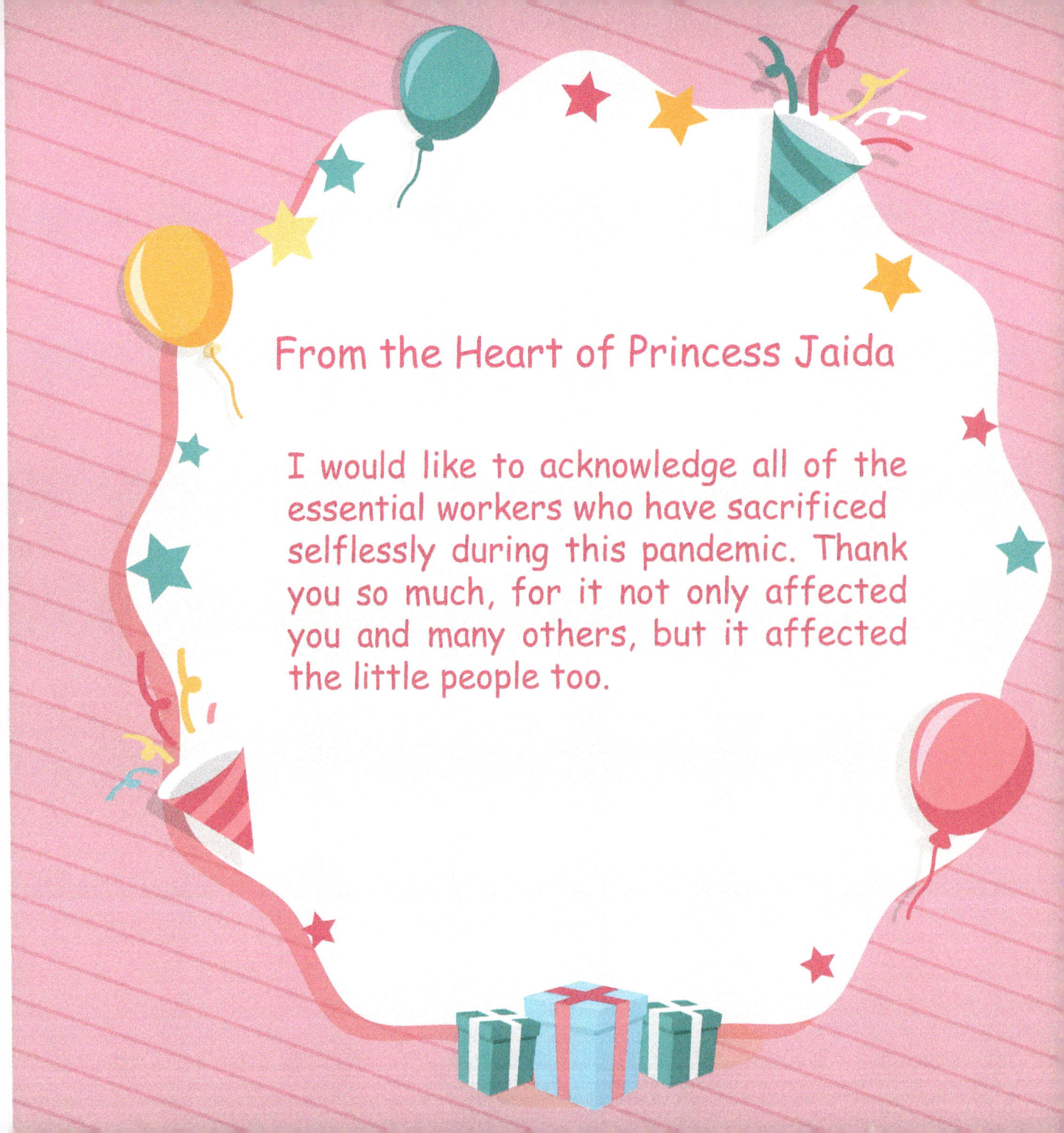

Author Bio

Jaida Lopez is not your average six year old. She is a loving, caring, charismatic little girl with big dreams. Jaida loves to draw, dance, play with her dolls, do arts and crafts, and Tik Tok. Jaida also loves to read and is now a published author.

Jaida is also an established pageant competitor and model. She competed and won the National Toddler Supreme with East Coast USA, and has also been crowned America's Miss Yankee with Cuoto Pageant Productions (2018 - 2019). Jaida has modeled for NY & NJ Fashion Week, EC Stars, and Toddlewood. She was born and resides in Brooklyn, New York with her mother and two brothers.

Always Dream Big!

www.ingramcontent.com/pod-product-compliance
Lightning Source LLC
Chambersburg PA
CBHW061129070526
44584CB00033B/4276